TABLE OF CONTENTS

INTRODUCTION

In a world where relationship status often defines our worth, it can be challenging for singles to connect with a world not aligning with a Biblical worldview. Whether navigating the dating scene, considering engagement, or choosing to remain single, it's vital to remember that true completeness does not come from a relationship status but from a deep, abiding relationship with Christ. Regardless of your age or background, God's plan for you is rich, fulfilling, and deeply meaningful, and He desires for you to experience the fullness of life found in Him alone.

These devotions are specifically designed for singles who are dating, about to be engaged, or are currently engaged to be married. Drawing from biblical wisdom and practical insights, each devotional aims to help you embrace your identity in Christ, find contentment in your current season, and live with purpose and joy. Whether dating, considering engagement, or focusing on your relationship with Jesus, these devotions will help you navigate your unique journey with faith and confidence.

As marriage becomes more likely, focus on your relationship with Jesus as the foundation for all other relationships. Marriage isn't the finish line. Your spouse will not complete you. Throughout these devotions, you will explore key themes such as understanding God's purpose for your life, cultivating a healthy mindset toward dating and relationships, and finding peace in God's timing. By focusing on your relationship with Christ, you will discover you are already complete, fully loved, and wholly accepted by the One who knows you best.

We pray that through these devotions, you are reminded of God's incredible love for you and that completeness is yours in Christ. May each devotion draw you closer to Him, strengthen your faith, and encourage you to live boldly and authentically, fully embracing your worth and identity in Christ and the possibility of someone joining you on the same journey. Remember, you are not alone—God is with you every step of the way, guiding, loving, and completing you in His perfect love. Your relationships will never fill a God-sized hole in your daily walk with the Lord; be complete in Christ.

"He must increase, but I must decrease." John 3:30

LET EVERYTHING FADE AWAY. In the old hymn "Turn Your Eyes Upon Jesus," it is stated that as we "look full in His wonderful face..." "the things of earth will grow strangely dim in the light of His glory and grace." The more we focus on Jesus, the easier it is to not focus on ourselves. The more we see the true heart and purpose of Jesus, the more we will desire to follow His purposes in our lives.

In his book *Mere Christianity*, C.S. Lewis wrote, "Humility is not thinking less of oneself but thinking of oneself less." One of the core truths of the Bible is summed up in the above verse, which quotes John the Baptist. Each day we set our eyes first on Jesus is a day spent decreasing so that His light, glory, and grace can shine through to the people we love and spend time around.

Takeaway: Focus more on Jesus than yourself. Spend more time talking about Jesus than talking about yourself.

How can you specifically decrease today and allow Jesus to increase in your heart and life?

What usually gets the most of your thoughts during the day? How does that reveal what's increasing in your life?

What would change in your relationships if everyone cared more about Jesus being seen than being noticed?

Blessed is the man who walks not in the counsel of the wicked, nor stands in the way of sinners, nor sits in the seat of scoffers; but his delight is in the law of the Lord, and on his law he meditates day and night. He is like a tree planted by streams of water that yields its fruit in its season, and its leaf does not wither. In all that he does, he prospers.
Psalms 1:1-3

PUT GOD FIRST. We put unrealistic and unhealthy expectations on our relationships. We wait and pray for God to provide someone we can grow old with. When a potential person (or even the thought of that person) grabs our attention, we can compromise who we are to become who we think they want us to be. The constant pressure of living up to a worldly identity is exhausting. We want to show others how much they mean to us, so we let them take precedence in our lives that we should set aside to follow God. What if there was a better way? Psalm 1 reminds us of the person who is grounded and firm, no matter their exterior circumstances. The person who seeks God's instructions and meditates on them. The people in your life need the best you—the you who is firm in your identity and who God has created you to be. Your family, friends, and maybe even your future spouse need someone who seeks God above all else.

Takeaway: You may not see immediate growth in this season of seeking God, but remember His promises: in the right season, the fruit will come.

What keeps you from seeking God first?

What are your thoughts about right now? Are you meditating on the things of God or the things of the world?

What part of God's instructions are you delighting in today?

Behold, God is my salvation; I will trust and will not be afraid; for the Lord God is my strength and my song, and he has become my salvation. Isaiah 12:2

THE "JESUS" STICKER. The belief that seeking to name, manifest, and claim something in your life will make it a reality can be destructive. Often, people engage in this practice because they view God as someone who is meant to serve their needs and requests. They believe that by invoking a magic formula of prayer, they can have whatever they want if they put the "Jesus" sticker on it. We sometimes try to do this in our dating and engagement by attempting to manifest a spouse from a dating relationship or by claiming a promise for ourselves in our engagement that doesn't reflect the blessing of God but rather our selfish desires.

When we come to Isaiah's writing in chapter 12, we see a different kind of speaking. This speech is not a claim to gain more material possessions. The context of this portion of Isaiah is set against the backdrop of trials and judgment that the people were experiencing. Yet, through this challenging moment, Isaiah didn't say he needed more material things to grow. He proclaimed (unlike manifesting) his trust in the Lord.

Takeaway: If you find yourself in a time of preparation for your next step in a relationship or even marriage, you do not need more material things at this moment; you need to trust in God's plan as you pursue Him together.

Isaiah's trust was proclaimed as tied to the Lord's salvation; how would you share in the same declaration?

What other things do you need to proclaim trust in God about in your current relationship?

Then Shaphan, the secretary, told the king, "Hilkiah, the priest has given me a book." And Shaphan read it before the king. When the king heard the words of the Book of the Law, he tore his clothes.
2 Kings 22:10-11

JUST A BOOK. For the last decade, one of the most successful shows has been those related to pawn shops. Typically, someone will bring an item to sell to a pawn shop owner. There are unique moments when someone brings an item they don't know its value or understand how much it is worth. After investigating the item or speaking with an expert, they discover an item worth much more than they initially assumed.

There was this moment in 2 Kings 22 when Shaphan, the secretary for King Josiah, had brought back The Book of the Law from Hilkiah. The way the language speaks in the passage is that he didn't realize what the book indeed was. To him, it was just a book. Yet when it began to be read, the realization that this was not just a book, but it was THE BOOK, the atmosphere completely changed.

Takeaway: In your dating life, especially as you grow older, you will be given opportunities to see Scripture as a book or the Book. Many couples will see dating as an area Scripture doesn't specifically address. So, they end up putting the principles of Scripture to the side, which can often lead to compromise or falling into temptation. Date with Scripture central to every decision made and see the work of God in your heart to bring them together for His purposes.

How have you been tempted to see Scripture as merely a book instead of The Book for your life?

How would it change how you date by keeping the truth of Scripture central to your relationship?

If you have experienced failure in relationships, what truths would Scripture teach you to help you start over again and do things God's way?

And he said to him, "You shall love the Lord your God with all your heart and with all your soul and with all your mind." Matthew 22:37

KINGDOM WORK-TOGETHER. Dating in today's world is not easy. Media and dating apps have created a dating culture of physical looks, sex, and finding the "perfect" person. Dating apps created this idea that there is always someone else out there. There are always more options. There is always the chance that you'll find someone more beautiful, funny, intelligent, adventurous -- whatever you're looking for, "Just keep swiping!" For Christians looking for a spouse, the dating scene can get discouraging. So, how do we live rooted in the Lord while dating? First, we must love the Lord our God with our entire being. This means that when we love the Lord wholeheartedly, we are actively seeking after Him. If we are actively seeking after Him, then we are reading His Word, listening to His voice, seeking His wisdom. One of the most important decisions we make in life is who we marry. This is because it has significant implications for our life's direction. Dating intentionally and rooted in the Lord keeps our focus on the purpose of dating -- finding a partner for Kingdom work. Let us choose to keep our eyes on the Lord and stand up for righteousness and purity while we are dating.

Takeaway: Loving the Lord wholeheartedly keeps our eyes fixed on finding a partner to do the work of the Kingdom. We do this with our hearts, seeing that our motivation for loving the Lord is not to find a spouse but to seek Christ. We do this with our souls, growing in our fellowship with the Lord. We do this with our minds (and bodies), pursuing purity in our thoughts and actions.

Which one of these have you seen hard to stay focused on during your dating experiences: heart, soul, mind (and body)?

How could being more in God's Word and prayer help you through your dating experiences?

What does it look like to choose Godliness in today's dating culture?

Therefore, as God's chosen ones, holy and dearly loved, put on compassion, kindness, humility, gentleness, and patience, bearing with one another and forgiving one another if anyone has a grievance against another. Just as the Lord has forgiven you, you are also to forgive. Above all, put on love, the perfect bond of unity.
Colossians 3:12-14

CHOOSE FORGIVENESS. Many mistakes are made in relationships, big ones and small ones. When we choose our spouse, we select someone imperfect with many weaknesses. Forgiveness no longer holds any sin against a person. Paul urges us to "bear with one another," which means patiently taking grievances and forgiving. When we live our lives aligning with God and putting on compassion, kindness, humility, gentleness, and patience, forgiveness becomes second nature. For your spouse to feel reconnected, they need to feel forgiven. We've all hurt someone, and we know the difference in how we think about whether we've been forgiven or not. Forgiveness reunites the bond that was created when you chose your person.

Takeaway: Forgiveness is difficult, but it is so powerful. Forgiveness is not a feeling you wait for, it's a choice you make. When you forgive as Christ forgave you, you protect unity, heal connection, and reflect the love God has already poured out on you.

Do you remember the last time you were forgiven?

Have you forgiven as the Lord has forgiven you?

How restorative did it feel to the relationship?

Trust in the Lord with all your heart, and do not lean on your own understanding. In all your ways, acknowledge him, and he will make straight your paths... Proverbs 3:5-6

INVITE GOD. Dating can be both exciting and daunting. As you navigate this journey, remember that prayer is a vital companion. It's a way to invite God into your relationships, helping you discern His will and find peace in the process.

Begin each day with a simple prayer, asking for wisdom and guidance in your dating life. Pray for clarity in your intentions and the right person to enter your life at the right time. Trust that God knows your desires and has a perfect relationship plan.

When you face challenges—whether communication issues or differing values—turn to prayer for strength and patience. Ask God to soften your heart and help you see your partner through His eyes. This perspective fosters empathy and understanding.

Also, pray together with your partner. Sharing your spiritual lives can deepen your connection and establish a strong foundation. It allows you both to grow individually and as a couple, inviting God into your shared journey.

Takeaway: Remember, dating is not just about finding "the one" but also about growing closer to God and becoming the best version of yourself. Through prayer, you can navigate this beautiful journey with faith and grace, trusting in God's perfect timing.

What specific qualities or values are you seeking in a partner, and how can prayer help you discern if someone aligns with those attributes?

How can you invite God into your dating life, individually and as a couple, to ensure your relationship honors Him?

How can you use prayer to navigate challenges or uncertainties in your dating journey, and how might it change your perspective on those situations?

"Look carefully then how you walk, not as unwise but as wise, making the best use of the time because the days are evil." Ephesians 5:15-16

OPPOSITE OF "ME" CULTURE. Serving others has become a foreign concept in our "me" first culture. You can donate a dollar for a need that catches your attention, but sacrificing daily for the betterment of others seems like overkill. A temptation arising in singleness is being unable to move past the "me" to a "we" in your thinking. Paul reminds us in Ephesians to pay careful attention to your walk as you consistently make the most of every day. You can get so caught up regretting past decisions or looking to the future that you miss out on opportunities to serve God and others today. Your spiritual health today matters. You must intentionally allow God to fill you up so you can pour into others. The battles of this life are too much for you to keep trying to do it under your strength. Pay careful attention today as to how you are walking with God.

Takeaway: Being intentional about seeking God daily not only helps you but also helps you engage better with others around you. Be present in this current season to see how you can serve others.

What "time thieves" are keeping you from serving in this season?

How are you making the most of this season?

What are two ways you can serve others today?

And he said to him, "You shall love the Lord your God with all your heart, soul, and mind. This is the great and first commandment. And a second is like it: You shall love your neighbor as yourself. Matthew 22:37-39

RELATIONSHIPS. Our ultimate goal in dating and all relationships should be to honor God. Whether it's a romantic relationship, friendship, or family dynamic, we are called to reflect Christ's love and truth. Pursuing relationships with purity, integrity, and intentionality is essential in dating. Hebrews 13:4 says, "Let marriage be held in honor among all." This applies not just to marriage but to dating and all relationships. Honor and respect should guide every interaction. Matthew 22:37-39 tells us, "Jesus replied: 'Love the Lord your God with all your heart and with all your soul and with all your mind. This is the first and greatest commandment. And the second is like it: Love your neighbor as yourself.'"

In all relationships, we are called to love others as Christ has loved us, prioritizing love for God above all.

Remember that God is the author of all relationships. Seek His guidance, commit to His standards, and trust that He will direct your steps in love and truth. Putting God first allows all our other relationships to fall into place as ordained. Seek God as your first relationship and let His easy path to provide you with the much-needed rest your soul needs.

Takeaway: Seek God's will in all your relationships, honoring Him in how you love others.

How can you honor God in your current relationships?

What steps can you take to align your dating life with biblical principles?

How are you trying to balance all the relationships in your life?

For everything, there is a season, and a time for every matter under heaven... Ecclesiastes 3:1

LONGING FOR "SOMEDAY." Dating in today's world can be challenging, especially for Christians. People share dating horror stories, from dates expecting too much physical contact to being catfished, ghosted, and left brokenhearted. Finding a Godly spouse can be much more complex than anticipated.

So, how does a Christian find hope in the prospect of a Godly marriage and family? In Ecclesiastes, King Solomon reminds us that everything has a time and season. Marriage is a beautiful gift from God. Although the dating season may be challenging, we can trust in the ultimate sovereignty of God's plan, knowing that every season has its purpose. If this is the season we are in, we can trust that it has meaning. While it's natural to long for the "someday" of marriage, we can also appreciate the process and recognize the personal growth during this time.

Takeaway: There is a season and a time for everything, and each season has a purpose. God is not delaying your life, He is developing it. This season, even if it's hard, is purposeful, intentional, and held securely in His time.

How does remembering that there is a time for everything give you hope for "someday"?

What can you do in this season to bring God glory?

When is it most challenging to remember you in a season, not a destination?

Do not move the ancient landmark that your fathers have set. Do you see a man skillful in his work? He will stand before kings; he will not stand before obscure men. Proverbs 22:28-29

TIGHTROPE WALKING. Tightrope walking is one of those feats that amazes me. First, the strength it takes to sustain oneself is fantastic. Then, to see someone balance themselves on just this tiny rope is somewhat unbelievable. There are even people who do tightrope walks outside during terrible wind conditions. The best acts are often when we see tightrope walkers without a net underneath them, just walking no matter what is below.

When it comes to how we treat the physical nature of our dating relationships, we like to act like tightrope walkers. Often, as believers, we will try to hold this balance between what is defined as sex versus what is considered physical engagement. Then, we will let the expectations of our culture be the winds that stir around our dating relationship so that we allow physicality to be justified and know if everything feels right. This justification is often done without considering what is below if we fall off the wire and succumb to temptation.

Takeaway: The writer of Proverbs knew that some things are to be established and left alone by God's grace. Some landmarks give us pause for why they are there. And we know that God doesn't want them moved. Instead, we can learn from them and keep them as a part of growing our obedience to the Lord.

What specific boundaries have you set for yourself to avoid sexual temptation, and how do you hold yourself accountable to them?

What common triggers or situations make you more susceptible to temptation? How do you navigate these situations?

How can we build healthy, non-sexual relationships with others while being single? What does that look like in practice?

Beloved, do not be surprised at the fiery trial when it comes upon you to test you as though something strange were happening to you.
1 Peter 4:12

FINDING HOPE IN SUFFERING. Have you ever navigated a giant maze? For those who could be better with directions, hitting dead ends and being confined by walls can be incredibly frustrating. Similarly, dating can be a maze of hope and excitement but comes with trials and heartache. As single Christians, we might experience suffering after investing our hearts in a relationship that doesn't turn out as we hoped. Remember the wisdom of 1 Peter 4:12 in these moments: "Beloved, do not be surprised at the fiery trial when it comes upon you to test you, as though something strange were happening to you."

Suffering in the aftermath of a relationship can feel disorienting and painful. Yet, Peter reminds us that these trials are not unexpected or beyond God's control. They are part of the refining process that can deepen our faith and character. God uses these experiences to teach us resilience, patience, and a greater dependence on Him.

As you navigate the pain of post-dating challenges, lean into God's comfort and grace. Use this time to reflect on what you've learned and how you've grown. Seek solace in prayer, community, and the promises of Scripture, reminding us that God is near the brokenhearted and saves those who are crushed in spirit (Psalm 34:18).

Takeaway: Embrace this season as an opportunity for spiritual growth and deeper intimacy with God. Trust that He is working through your suffering to produce a greater good and prepare you for the future He has in store for you.

How have you seen relationships change you? For good or bad?

Have you let some of these experiences affect your current relationship?

How can you give God the glory and grow closer to Him?

For because he himself has suffered when tempted, he is able to help those who are being tempted.
Hebrews 2:18

MASONRY IS MORE FINAL. "Masonry seems like hard work. It isn't harder; it's just more final... Once you make that first cut into the stone, it can't be undone. It sets in motion a series of choices. What used to be a shapeless block of limestone or granite begins its long transformation journey and will never be the same." – The Chosen, Season 1, Episode 5.

Temptation is something every human being faces and will walk through. Temptation itself is not a sin, but giving oneself over to temptation results in sin. This is because, like masonry, sin is final. When facing temptation, it cannot be undone; once a person gives into temptation to sin, it cannot be undone. Everyone's decision sets a series of choices and changes that cannot be undone. Temptation is a constant battle; no one will be completely free from temptation in this life. However, men and women can be encouraged in the truth because Jesus Christ faced temptation, and there is hope in this life. Hope only comes from Jesus. Hope can bring encouragement to face temptation and restore what is broken. There is hope all can find in Jesus. Once this hope in the free gift of salvation through Jesus is accepted, a long transformation journey begins where one becomes more like Christ, and he or she will never be the same.

Takeaway: Temptation itself is a natural part of life, but succumbing to it can lead to sin, which has irreversible consequences. The hope found in Jesus Christ offers encouragement and transformation, helping individuals resist temptation and grow more like Him.

How can understanding the distinction between temptation and sin help make better decisions and maintain personal integrity?

How might being in a committed relationship influence a person's approach to temptation and boundaries?

How does the hope and transformation offered by Jesus Christ help individuals deal with temptation and navigate their spiritual journey?

Let us then with confidence draw near to the throne of grace, that we may receive mercy and find grace to help in time of need. Hebrews 4:16

NOT PERFECT. The writer of Hebrews uses the phrase "let us" throughout the book. He encourages his readers to understand that they are not alone and that God has a plan for them. God's plan operates through His grace and mercy. We are called to be obedient and follow what His word tells us to do. By doing so, as the verse says, we can have confidence in drawing near to the Lord at His throne of grace.

From His throne, come the grace and mercy necessary for the seasons of dating and engagement. For those who are dating, they need both to receive grace and to show grace as they learn more about each other. Remember, the other person in a dating relationship is not perfect, so showing grace is essential in the early stages of the relationship. Grace should also be present in your preparation for those who are engaged. Despite the many books and manuals available, they cannot replace the lessons learned through experience.

Takeaway: Through all the dating and engaged moments, God's grace helps us in the good times and bad. It grows and sustains us. It keeps us and teaches us.

What did you recently ask your partner or future spouse to show grace with you about? How did it encourage you to grow together?

What are some of your most significant needs in your current relationship status? How will seeking God's grace first help you in these situations?

Let love be genuine. Abhor what is evil; hold fast to what is good. Love one another with brotherly affection. Outdo one another in showing honor.
Romans 12:9-10

WHAT IS HONOR? It's pretty human to want to "outdo" others or not be "outdone" by someone else. Middle School is probably the time we all were the worst at this, am I right? Trying to prove something about yourself and ensuring people didn't make fun of you. There is also one friend who is a story topper, meaning they always have a story to follow up someone else's story that is better than the one just told. We all eye-roll that friend most of the time. Topping or outdoing someone else generally comes from a place of insecurity. Paul flips the thinking on outdoing one another.

"Outdo one another in showing honor." Instead of outdoing others to prove you are better than them, what would happen if you went above and beyond in showing respect and care? Redeem the naturally sinful notion of being better than someone by putting them above and before yourself.

Takeaway: Be the best at intentionally putting others before yourself. When love is real and rooted in what is good, honor becomes a daily decision to put someone else first without needing anything in return.

Who in your life do you need to be more intentionally respectful towards?

What do you need to shift your daily thinking to be more intentional about honoring people around you?

And rising very early in the morning, while it was still dark, he departed and went out to a desolate place, and there he prayed. Mark 1:35

FOLLOWING JESUS. It's common for people to feel excited when they start dating someone new. We often rearrange our schedules and set aside as much time as possible to spend with and talk to this person. Getting to know them becomes a top priority.

What if we approached our relationship with Jesus in the same way? Imagine if we rearranged our schedules, dedicated as much time as possible to Him, and made Jesus a priority. One way to connect with Jesus is to visit a coffee shop, bring a journal and Bible, turn off the phone, and be with Him. In those moments, focus on learning more about Him without distractions. The more we invest time in getting to know Jesus, the better equipped we become to serve Him and others, and the more we grow to reflect His character.

Takeaway: Following Jesus' example of retreating to spend time alone with the Lord, we cultivate a deeper relationship with Him. This intentional time with Him helps us better understand His teachings, align our lives with His will, and become more like Him.

Is spending time with Jesus the most important use of our time?

What can you do this week to prioritize and maximize your time with Jesus?

How can we remember Jesus is with us every day, all day?

And whatever you do, in word or deed, do everything in the name of the Lord Jesus, giving thanks to God the Father through him. Colossians 3:17

DWELLING IN THE LORD. In the hustle and bustle of modern dating, it is easy to get swept up in emotions, expectations, and the pursuit of companionship. Yet, as we seek to honor God in every area of life, we must ask, "How would God have me rest in Him as I pursue a relationship with another?"

Jesus charges us to "seek first the kingdom of God and his righteousness, and all these things will be provided for you." And "don't worry about tomorrow, because tomorrow will worry about itself. Each day has enough trouble of its own." (Mt 6:33)

So, as we seek the many good gifts He has given His people, like dating, let us remember that these pursuits begin with an intimate, personal relationship with Him. Your identity and worth are found in Christ, not your relationship status. Root yourself in His love and truth, and then see how it transforms every relationship you have.

Paul instructs, "And whatever you do, in word or deed, do everything in the name of the Lord Jesus, giving thanks to God the Father through him." (Col. 3:17). Even your dating life is called to be an act of worship. It's about seeking a partner who stokes and encourages your faith and points you to the glory of God. So, as you desire to be rooted in Christ, reflect His love, grace, and truth to the world, even in your dating life.

Takeaway: Seek first the Kingdom and His righteousness, and as you tread this beautiful and often difficult path, you will experience His peace and blessing in a way that truly honors Him.

How would God have me rest in Him as I pursue a relationship with another?

How can you make sure your dating life or engagement is glorifying God?

But the wisdom from above is first pure, then peaceable, gentle, open to reason, full of mercy and good fruits, impartial and sincere. James 3:17

FOREVER "THE ONE". It's easy to get so caught up in choosing the right person and looking outward that we forget to take a good look inward. Not only are you deciding if this person is right for you, but they, too, will decide if you are right for them. When we can apply the wisdom God has given us and apply it to ourselves first, it shifts our perspective on what we are looking for in someone to date and marry. Fix yourself first. Look to James 3 as a guide to the kind of spouse you want to be and the one you want to look for as a part of your future. You can make decisions that bring inner peace and are merciful and unwavering while showing compassion and patience. It is prudent to know what core values are instilled in you and what values you expect of your future mate. Thankfully, our sweet Father will guide us in our steps and give us wisdom in small decisions like finding your mate.

Takeaway: God will give you the wisdom to make life-altering and exciting decisions like finding your spouse! While seeking our Father's knowledge, we should also live in obedience, displaying compassion, kindness, humility, gentleness, and patience.

What are your core values?

How can you live by these core values?

How will you use these values to choose a mate?

Do not be unequally yoked with unbelievers. For what partnership has righteousness with lawlessness? Or what fellowship has light with darkness? *2 Corinthians 6:14*

FAITH IN MY DATING LIFE. Throughout Scripture, the term "dating" is not used. In Biblical times, parents typically set up marriage and began with "betrothal," which meant engagement. So, in 2 Corinthians 6, in verse 14, Paul discusses not being yoked with those who do not believe in God. Paul refers to Old Testament law stating that a donkey and an ox should not be yoked together in the fields. The Lord said this because an ox is stronger and more likely to carry the bulk of the load, while the donkey is stubborn and unreliable. If these two animals plowed the field together, the field would end up unevenly plowed, making the ground for seeds to be planted unstable. The same is true in our relationships today, whether in business partners, friendships, or, yes - dating relationships. As you choose someone to date, choose someone who is evenly yoked with you. When we are yoked with believers, we can plant seeds for the Kingdom of the Lord and have faith that God will make those seeds grow.

Takeaway: When we choose someone to date, how they exercise their faith shows how they will treat those around them. If they lack faith, they will act obstinately and antagonistically toward the things of the Lord. However, if they have true faith, they will find ways to partner for the gospel's sake, no matter what! Therefore, choose someone who desires to work and plant seeds for the Lord.

How does the illustration about the ox and the donkey make you feel about your dating relationships?

Why do people sometimes wait to discuss faith in dating?

Whyshouldarelationshipwithsomeonewhodemonstrates faith be conditional when pursuing any next steps?

What does it look like to have faith in your dating relationships?

Let us then with confidence draw near to the throne of grace, that we may receive mercy and find grace to help in time of need. *2 Peter 3:9*

FLEAS VERSUS FEVER. Augustine says, "Present fleas are always deemed worse than past fevers." When it comes to areas of our lives where we try to hold onto the past, if we aren't careful, these can become nagging fleas. Here's the thing about fleas: typically, other people don't see them flying around us, nor do they hear them in our ears.

How true this is of guilt in our lives! Guilt is often something other people don't see or even know to look for. We can be adept at masking our guilt instead of surrendering it to the Lord. Furthermore, when we carry guilt, we hear the message of the enemy saying, "You need to keep holding on to this. You can't let it go. You will never be forgiven." When we carry guilt, shame, and regrets from our pasts, we soon join in, and before long, we don't just listen—we believe what the enemy says. Peter was adamant in showing his readers that God doesn't see our guilt as something to hold against us. He sees it as something from which He wants to free us. This is why He is so patient and slow to anger, so we will willingly give it to Jesus.

Takeaway: The present is a great time to know that the Lord desires our relationships not to carry guilt. Rather in repentance, we can be set free from our past!

What can be indications of someone bringing guilt into a dating relationship?

For those who are engaged, why should this be addressed in your preparation before you are married?

How is it encouraging to know that the Lord is patient with us, even when we try to carry our own guilt?

Humble yourselves, therefore, under the mighty hand of God so that at the proper time He may exalt you. 1 Peter 5:6

HUMILITY FOUND IN CHRIST. Dating can be humbling, like presenting a dish on a cooking show. You're confident in your creation, but the judge's tastes may differ, leaving you with a polite smile instead of the praise you hoped for. It's a reminder that personal preferences vary, no matter how well you prepare. Therefore, in the pursuit of a meaningful relationship, single Christians often face a blend of hope and anxiety. We desire companionship and seek to honor God in the process, but sometimes, our expectations or fears can lead us to forget the foundational principle of humility.

1 Peter 5:6 reminds us to humble ourselves under God's mighty hand. This verse calls us to trust His timing and plan rather than pushing our agenda or striving for control. In dating, this means approaching relationships with a heart of service and openness rather than one of entitlement or self-focus. Humility in dating involves recognizing that our value and identity are found in Christ, not our relationship status. It means surrendering our desires and anxieties to God and acknowledging He knows what's best for us. As we step into the dating world, let us seek to reflect Christ's love by being genuine, kind, and patient. Humility allows us to approach potential partners with respect and without undue pressure, and it also prepares us to accept God's will for our lives with grace, whether it leads to a relationship or not.

Takeaway: Humility isn't a sign of weakness but a strength that aligns us with God's perfect plan. Trust in His timing and embrace the process with faith.

Where are you finding your value?

How are you showing your identity in Christ while dating?

What steps must you take to build humility in your relationships?

Not that we are sufficient in ourselves to claim anything as coming from us, but our sufficiency is from God. *2 Corinthians 3:5*

INSUFFICIENT & UNFULFILLED. Whether you have been waiting only a little while or for years for the right person to come along, you probably have some hopes and expectations for your relationship—and feeling loneliness is not one of them. If loneliness creeps in, you may wonder if something is wrong or broken in your relationship.

Look at 2 Corinthians 3:5. It says we (all people) are not sufficient on our own. We cannot gather, work for, or manipulate ourselves or anything else to truly fulfill our needs. That may seem like life is meaningless and frustrating. But there is hope! Our sufficiency comes through Christ, not another person, a relationship, or material goods.

How does this relate to loneliness? If you cannot be sufficient, neither can the person you are dating. And, neither of you is meant to be sufficient for each other either. At times, they will disappoint you. They may not be able to be there for you in the way that you want, leaving you feeling lonely and unsatisfied. Christ promises never to leave or forsake you. He alone is all-powerful and sufficient to meet our needs.

Takeaway: Don't look to the person you are dating to fulfill God's place. Seek the Lord daily, and He will give you joy and peace. When you feel lonely, pray and call upon the Lord before going to another person. Remember, our sufficiency comes through an active relationship with our good and gracious Lord, who is always with us.

When you are feeling lonely, who do you turn to first? Try praying and praising the Lord for His goodness before talking with your significant other.

Do you depend on your relationship to feel sufficient or fulfilled? If yes, ask the Lord to help you look to Him for satisfaction and joy.

How can a young man keep his way pure? By guarding it according to your word. Psalm 119:9

THE PATH OF PURITY. When purity in dating comes up, sexual purity is usually the first thought, which is undeniably important. However, purity in dating encompasses more than just sexual boundaries. Psalm 119:9 teaches us to maintain purity by aligning our lives with God's Word. So, how can we stay pure in today's dating relationships? It starts with immersing ourselves in Scripture. By living in accordance with the Lord's teachings, our relationships become healthier and reflect His character. We embody qualities such as patience, kindness, joy, servanthood, generosity, forgiveness, and grace. These traits mirror the Lord's pure relationship with His bride, the church. By pursuing purity in all aspects of our dating lives—both sexual and otherwise—we lay the groundwork for a strong, God-pleasing relationship. This holistic approach to purity honors God and fosters a deeper, more meaningful connection with our partner.

Takeaway: Remaining pure in dating relationships begins with being in God's word, so we mirror His character. Purity is not just about what you avoid, but who you are becoming in Christ. It is God's word that guards your heart and shapes your choices

What are ways you can ensure you are actively in God's word?

Does being in God's word encourage you to be more like him? Why or why not?

So then you are no longer strangers and aliens, but you are fellow citizens with the saints and members of the household of God, built on the foundation of the apostles and prophets, Christ Jesus himself being the cornerstone, in whom the whole structure, being joined together, grows into a holy temple in the Lord. In Him, you also are being built together into a dwelling place for God by the Spirit. Ephesians 2:19-22

CHURCH= COMMUNITY & ACCOUNTABILITY.

The online dating world has become the norm for meeting people in our culture. From these platforms that suggest compatibility, there comes a moment when you begin to engage in conversation. As your circles collide, you integrate each other's presence into the communities you have created. Here, the church can become valuable for your dating and engaged relationships.

From a dating perspective, you both need godly accountability to help you learn more about each other in an environment that fosters spiritual connection before moving toward physical connection in marriage. From an engaged perspective, you must establish a community encouraging spiritual growth as you prepare to become a husband and wife. Both aspects of accountability and community look different if the connections you make occur outside the church. The world has an entirely different perspective on relationships compared to the teachings of the Lord. Therefore, you need the body of Christ—other redeemed individuals who can help you build each other up!

Takeaway: The church is to be the people where connections can be fostered and grown with accountability and community for dating and engaged couples.

Who from church can help foster accountability in your life? How would this help you in a dating relationship?

Who can help you walk through establishing community as an engaged couple?

Why is mentorship valuable to what you do during this season? What about after your wedding day?

But in your hearts honor Christ the Lord as holy, always being prepared to make a defense to anyone who asks you for a reason for the hope that is in you; yet do it with gentleness and respect.
1 Peter 3:15

SHARING THE GOSPEL. There are moments at the beginning of a relationship or when you get engaged and feel bombarded with questions. For a new dating relationship, these questions might be, "How did you meet?" or "What attracted you to them?" When you get engaged, the questions shift to "When did you know they were the one?" or "Have you set a date yet?" Let's be honest—some even come with weirdness, such as "What do you see in that person?" or "What took you so long?" Often, we might feel tempted to respond in anger in those moments.

Similarly, Peter shares that when our hearts are focused on living for the Lord, no matter what stage we find ourselves in, we should expect to be asked questions. These might be more like, "Why do you believe the Bible?" or "Why is your hope in Jesus Christ?" Whatever the question, you should be prepared to give an answer—not for the sake of getting into an argument, but to respond, as Peter writes, with gentleness and respect. One pastor said, "The gospel is offensive, but you don't have to be."

Takeaway: Being set apart for Christ naturally invites questions. When they come, our response should reflect both truth and love, confidence in the gospel paired with the kindness of Christ.

Can you think of more awkward questions that come up when you are dating? Or newly engaged?

How would you answer the question of where your hope is? Why should it not be in your partner or future spouse?

Do you know why you believe the Bible, not just that you believe the Bible?

Be kind to one another, tenderhearted, forgiving one another, as God in Christ forgave you.
Ephesians 4:32

PURSUING RECONCILIATION. Entering the dating world can be a transformative experience, but it also offers the opportunity for significant personal growth. Before stepping into a new relationship, it's crucial to examine our hearts and ensure we're prepared for the emotional and spiritual demands of dating. Ephesians 4:32 offers timeless wisdom for this journey: "Be kind to one another, tenderhearted, forgiving one another, as God in Christ forgave you."

Reconciliation and forgiveness are essential elements of a healthy relationship, and they start with us. If there are unresolved conflicts or lingering grudges from past relationships or personal interactions, it's essential to address these before pursuing a new romantic connection. The reality is that holding grudges is like carrying a backpack full of rocks. Every time you add another grudge, the load gets heavier, making each step more burdensome. Letting go of grudges is like emptying that backpack, lightening your load, and making your journey through life much more enjoyable and unrestricted. Therefore, holding onto past hurts can cloud our judgment and hinder our ability to enter a relationship with a pure and open heart.

Takeaway: Seek reconciliation with those you've hurt or who have hurt you. This doesn't mean you restore every relationship to its former state, but strive to release bitterness and extend forgiveness where possible. By doing so, you align yourself with God's call to love and kindness, enabling you to approach new relationships with grace and understanding.

What relationships do you need to ask God to help you forgive and mend so you can step into a new relationship free from past baggage and ready to build something beautiful in His love?

What part of Ephesians 4:32 challenges you the most right now?

Are you entering relationships hoping someone else will heal wounds that God is asking you to address first?

By this all people will know that you are my disciples, if you have love for one another.
John 13:35

LOVE FOR ONE ANOTHER. There are famous lyrics from the song that say, "I want to know what love is." In the song, the person is confused about what true love is supposed to look like because of heartache. But when it comes to loving again, they want to make sure that the love they experience is true and from a pure heart.

When it comes to defining the nature of love, we often struggle. We bring the baggage of past relationships, scars, and breakups to our next relationship, trying to convince ourselves that it will be better. This is where Jesus' words ring so powerfully true. We can begin to express the most authentic nature of love not by how the world defines it or even how we define it ourselves. True love begins in Christ and then continues through us! Jesus was adamant that the world would only experience His love through those who truly follow Him.

Takeaway: Instead of letting past heartaches define how we love, we can choose to love from a place of healing and renewal rooted in the love of Christ. True love begins with Him and becomes a testimony of His grace to those around.

What feels like baggage you are trying to carry around today in relationships?

What are ways you can be known for the love you have for Jesus with others?

Oh give thanks to the Lord, for he is good, for his steadfast love endures forever! Psalm 107:1

CULTIVATING GRATITUDE. In Arkansas, there are mines where people can dig for diamonds on their own. What people are trying to do is to find a hidden gem that can become a treasure. In navigating relationships, it's easy to become preoccupied with what is happening or what we wish were different. However, Psalm 107:1 calls us to have a different perspective: "Oh give thanks to the Lord, for he is good, for his steadfast love endures forever!"

As single Christians, cultivating an attitude of gratitude can transform our dating experience. Instead of focusing solely on finding the "perfect" partner or the next step, we are invited to appreciate and thank God for His goodness in every aspect of our lives. Gratitude shifts our focus from what is lacking to the blessings we already have.

Being thankful during the dating process means recognizing the growth, lessons, and joys. It involves thanking God for the relationships and experiences that shape us, even if they don't lead to the outcomes we initially hoped for. Each date, each conversation, and even each heartbreak can serve as a step in our journey of faith and personal development.

Takeaway: In your dating journey, take time to reflect on and give thanks for the ways God is working in your life. Trust His steadfast love guides and shapes you, even when the path seems unclear.

List three hidden gems you are grateful to God for giving you in your relationship.

How have these made you a more Christlike person?

Can you step into a new relationship free from past baggage and ready to build something beautiful in His love?

But God shows his love for us in that while we were still sinners, Christ died for us. Romans 5:8

UNCONDITIONAL LOVE. "If they..." We put conditions on our relationships with the people around us, but the love we are called to imitate is God's unconditional love. The biggest thing that holds most of us back from really feeling accepted by God is the fact that we ourselves do not give unconditional love. We put conditions on the relationships around us and live like God does the same thing to us.

It is true that our relationship with God is better when we follow His commands. It is also true that to really be in relationship with God we must first repent of our sins and believe in Jesus. However, these are not conditions of God's love or at least His heart for our redemption. God FIRST loved us, while we were still sinners. At our worst, God loves. At our darkest, God loves. At our most insecure, God loves. In moments where we do not feel accepted, it is our heart that needs to be checked and questioned, not Gods. Since God is the same from beginning to the end of time, His love never changes and never fails. It is you and I that need to seek Him with all our heart and He promises we will find Him.

Takeaway: Through Jesus' sacrifice, you are accepted by God regardless of how you "feel" at any given moment. Your acceptance rests on Jesus' finished work, not your feelings or faithfulness.

3

Do you live in God's love and acceptance or in your own insecurities?

Make a list of at least three ways God has shown His love and acceptance to you. (Hint: Jesus' sacrifice is the biggest one.)

Nevertheless, each person should live as a believer in whatever situation the Lord has assigned to them, just as God has called them.
1 Corinthians 7:17

COMPLETE IN CHRIST. We live in a world where envy is common. For example, two friends are jealous of each other for opposite lives. One friend is envious of the other friend who has a husband and a child, while the friend with the husband and child envies the single friend's ability to enjoy spontaneous fun with friends. In 1 Corinthians 7, Paul addresses the church in Corinth about the blessings and gifts of single and married life. He reminds us that each situation is a blessing from God. Often, we become so fixated on what we wish we had that we forget that God ordains our current circumstances. There can be a deep desire to be a wife and a mother or a husband and a father, which can sometimes be painful. However, remind yourself that you are in this place for a reason.

In verse 17, Paul emphasizes that we should live as believers regardless of our life circumstances. Therefore, when dating, we should strive to live as Jesus did and seek a partner who shares this commitment. Although each person is complete in Jesus, our relationships should reflect this completeness. This starts by recognizing and accepting our current position as determined by the Lord and living our lives in alignment with Jesus' example.

Takeaway: We are complete in Jesus, no matter our relationship status, whenever we live our lives as a believer in Jesus should.

Are you living your life so that others can see Jesus in you?

What emotions surface when you think about your current season? contentment, frustration, gratitude, longing?

What pressures, internal or external, push you to rush into the next stage of life?